Open
after dark

Sue Proffitt

Oversteps Books

First published in 2017 by

Oversteps Books Ltd
6 Halwell House
South Pool
Nr Kingsbridge
Devon
TQ7 2RX
UK

www.overstepsbooks.com

Printed in Great Britain by imprint digital, Devon

for my mother, Jeannie,
and for Desirée, who sat beside me
through the longest night —
with my love.

Acknowledgements

Some of these poems have appeared in the following magazines and anthologies:

South, Artemis, Scintilla, Ariadne's Thread, Moor Poets Vol.III, The Book of Love and Loss, Confluence (poetry from the Two Rivers group), *Shoots* (Bath Spa University), *Torbay Poetry Competition 2009, The Virginia Warbey Poetry Competition 2010, Resurgence Poetry Competition 2015, The Broadsheet, Aesthetica 2016, Teignmouth Poetry Festival Competition 2016.*

I am indebted to Mark Cocker, author of *Crow Country* (Cape, 2007), for his permission to use the title for my poem.

Grateful thanks to Greta Stoddart and the Exeter poetry group to which I belong, and also to members of Litmus, for their support and encouragement with these poems.

Contents

Section Three: My Mother's Language

Section Four: To Make a Path

Section One: The Gift

The Gift

On the coast path
past the condemned cottages
tilting towards the sea
a frantic flapping —
young kestrel
in the open porch of one cottage
on a ledge facing the window,
beating herself against it again and again.

I recognise that panic
when the world blacks to this —

letmeoutletmeoutletmeout.

She was oblivious to me, to the open air behind her,
all she had to do was turn round.

I approached her (the wonder of it!)
cupped her drumming panic like a prayer
walked to the cliff-edge
opened my hands.

The planet paused on its axis
watched this wild thing
unmoving in my palms.

This was the gift she gave me
before she flew
so sudden,
no blink or breath to time it.

I stood there, the old grief
of separation returning —
my hands shivering
in a memory of feathers.

Fox

Something edge-on
sideways
half-hid figure in a dream
you see her
don't see her,
peering through the dark
for a thicker black
in the thicket of grasses
clicking their dry bones —
disturbing a scrape of stone.

In this held spell
this leakage of light
where all is seepage
and a slow filling-up — there —
in the sudden glare
of the lighthouse
two ears, pricked;
her stare guttural deep
in the stomach's pit.

The night splits
(for a breath held)
thickens back to black.

Ursus Maritimus

In June 2008 a starving polar bear swam more than 200 miles to reach
Iceland, and was shot on arrival in case it posed a threat to humans.

Across the radar screen of polar dark
a pulse of bear —
stubborn entity moving south.

Navigating instinct,
the dream of blood warm in your maw,
its metal current on your tongue
pulling you mile
                 after mile

bear-white, dark water
batting paws
beneath the sea's heave
slowed down to the trudging compass
of your heart.

Dragging your bulk upshore,
buffeted head nodding slowly
side to side,
the sodden weight of mottled fur
heavy ropes of skin
a drenched thing
calved from the haunch of mother-north,

did the tiniest flicker inside your ear
that hears seals breathe
miles below
murmur a warning?

Dark water, bear-white,
dragging your story behind you.

Wild Boar

Dusk. Under a slate sky
the forest is losing its edges.
Round, baffled faces
of chain-sawed stumps
loom through dense air.

I'm quickening my pace
a sound at my back
snap of twigs underfoot,
small explosions of spooked birds,
plop of nuts and seeds
something else —

wild boar.

No time to run. No stick. No dog.
From behind me they stampede
and the forest splinters apart,
the felled tree between heart and throat
trapping my breath.

Stuck like a pig to ground
I watch them thud alongside me
not dark like trees
or pale like the prisoners in concrete stalls
but rust, tusked to the hilt,
shrieks hot as wet metal tearing —
something hurtling through space unstoppable,
centuries colliding through the thickening dark
through my pummelling heart —
ripping the sealed drum of my ear open.

I watch them chasing each other
round the curve of the path.
The quiet, following after,
hovers outside me
ringing like a storm glass.

Encounter

What's this twist
              in the grass
                   spear-pattern
                        dragon's tail
                   green-toothed, gold
          gold-green —
stopped
     by you in my path,
               quick, quick
                    nerving away,
                         I don't want anyone
          to see you, scream
snake
          you pulse,
               boneless current,
                    muscle
                         pumping yourself
                              into the grass
                    and the grass opens
               for you, the grizzled grass
          divides like a sea
     divides like a room
of whiskered old men
     falling back from your
          sinewy shine
               as you dive,
                    taking your perfect knowledge
                         underground.

Butterfly

It couldn't fly
wings crumpled tissue
but still an eye —
vermilion, purple —
glared from each,
jewels stamped on a paper bag.
I gave it honey. Imagine,
the cold, the descending dark,
a banquet
but your mouth is locked.
I put it on a leaf
where it lay for three days.
Touched gently,
it would move a feeler,
maybe a leg, in slow motion.
It takes this long to let go.
A year later, I uncurl
its brittle shroud —
the shock of those eyes
un-emptied,
holding vigil over
a papyrus flight-map.

Jellyfish

What's a moon doing in this forest?
I hover above you, unseen but not unfelt
as you present your full face,
thin as transparent latex
brown and frilled as an old maid's cap
blotched purple, a flower.

How is a flower a lung?
shrinking in, ballooning out —
bellows   parasol
        parachute   moon-mouth —
my words slide off you
like rain off an umbrella.

I have seen you press yourself
against a vertical rope of weed
and stay there, as if thinking hard,
as if willing it to move,
then slide around it, viscous, untroubled,
trailing three, four feet behind you
poisoned filaments live as electricity.

And underneath?
Ruched skirts, creamy and crumpled
as a dropped wedding dress
hitched up again but unravelling
frayed trails, diaphanous frills
disintegrating threads.

What a marvel.
A moon in a wedding-dress.

Sea Holly

snag-spangling   spindrift spikelets
the shoreline   you dizzy
ouching fingers   the hummers zuzzing
shattering shingle   your molten centres
Bluelight stunners
in the thrusting   silver stormheads
oblivion-bang   you sing a cracking
of summer   open the cliff-face
a god-thrown fist   a thistle-ing hymn
of firecrackers   blue dervish-dancing

Bluebells

Overnight they arrive
pour down the flanks of slopes,
flooding the coast path.

This is a mystery.
Out of the blue
a carpet, landed

but the truth is
each bell dreams itself
in the womb

inches its green tube
through, then from the centre
something purple pushes —

the bell
fluted edges curving close
around white clappers.

They patch and pool
the hollows but further away
dissolve

blue breath,
a haze seen sideways,
the slide of the iris

from something manifest —
ghosts belling the earth
sea-air, thickened.

Take them on film,
they disappear.
Take them indoors,

something wilts
deep inside you.
The air detects a blue frequency.

Overnight they arrive.

Salmon Run

Not far now. Wet silver
sometimes black and lightless
becoming copper, iron on our lips

and we taste it. Home.

Over rocks, giddying water
fast and swollen like my belly
the urge to let go, let go

so strong

the magnetic undercurrent
of my beginning pulling on me
like a hook sunk deep

in my body

the river dragging us into dark
overhangs of reeds, grass,
sometimes I see a bird

watching us

hunger left far behind   –
I have darkened, thinned
to this pulse – something quickened

something quickening

inside me, the urgency
greater now – here it is,
the taste of my arriving

and we are returning

to ourselves
in this gravel's riffle
in this tail-beaten redd

I am unravelling in my thousands.

Sea-Watching

It is light breaking open a dark seam
through half-closed eyes:
sparks, but not where the dark
splits white.

It is the line, which is not a line
but a body, heavier than dark.
Light burns on the body,
surfs the heave,
the fall and rise,
the edge throwing off its veils.

It is the wet shine dizzying the sand,
percolation of light
through stones.

It is the cream curdling the grist
where pebbles gleam,
the fall and rise,
forward, retreat, the crack
splitting open muttering stones,
the knocked-back slap
of water on rock.

It is the tug back
deep in my groin
the release, the fall and rise
of blood, lymph,
this salt-mash alchemy
of gallons in a sac,
this circuitry called back —

it is the farmed salmon
sensing the wild ones
it cannot see swim home.

Kestrel at Start Point

Quivering wings
suspended
in a head-wind
held tremblingly still
the taut bow
of your body
poised to a point
arrowed
to a mouse move.
A clean clear curve
downwards,
closer still.
Such control
for the kill —
whatever it is
below you
cannot know
how close death hovers,
balancing on the breath
of unawareness,
the one false move
springing
dark extinction —
that golden stare
fixes on me,
and as I rifle
through my life
it's there —
neck-breath near.

The White Roebuck

In 2009 a rare white roebuck, believed to be a 'genetic throwback' to a much older species, was discovered on an estate in Scotland. A price was put on its head.

Genes have memories.
Here's a long spiral staircase winding down
into primordial dark, and on each step
an etch of what was, what might have been;
images shift under your feet
print themselves on your soles.

A long way down, there's a white gleam.
You can barely see it in the dark,
we're close to the forest on this part
of the spiral. Trees breach
the teeming soil, gargantuan,
into green sky. Creepers swing
fur ropes in your face,
everything drips. This is the birth-ooze
of the world, her postpartum
opening of waters.

It is here you might see him,
odd mothball-face
breaking through the dim soup
of leaves, breaking through
like a drowned man's face
breaks palely from the water
as he's heaved to the surface.

The white roebuck,
angel of the forest, jumping the tree creepers.
He is the foggy emblem,
deer-breath of the dark.
He is what appears, ghostly,
after you've left your heavy traces,
flattened ropes and tattered leaves,
walked slowly away from this dark space;

you don't look back, but on the back of your neck
something cool flares. Something
blots your skin in a pale compress.
Something white is looking through you
into the clearing.

Skylark at Terminal 5

Such a small sound
so clear

in the cracks between
white roars

air forced forwards
and backwards

split every forty-five seconds
a thin skin

and in between
something sings

thread-needle
chirrups and buzzes

holds its birdworld
intact

in a desert of hulked edges
a blasted sky

and empties itself
into a pure space

where a small sound of roaring
fades.

Crow Country

I am full of crows.
With a fish-eye lens
I look in on them,
black stigmata.

They flew across my vision
scoring a black script
hard and fine as a scalpel
over my pupils,

shot into a tree —
instantly disembodied
into branch, twig, leaf.
This was the one bright moment.

I know they will sit
on a sick lamb's flank
peer closely, consider
its mewling and

peck out its eyes,
take into themselves despair
like a dark cud
until it hardens, gleams

like a lump of obsidian.
I love their pitilessness —
so clear, clean.
They've arrived for a reason.

My whole world contracts
like a marble inside their eyes.

Murmuration

Inert at my wheel
straining upwards,
my solitary trajectory braked,
I am such a lumpish thing.

It's all happening up there
in a mackerel-shine —
the crackling synapses
of a thousand bird-brains

opening up the dawn,
sieving the half-light,
descending
in a shivering drift

embossing a tree in black,
every branch starling'd.

Water Boatmen

Meniscus-skaters
each one two
joined at the feet

pinpricking the water's skin
in a staccato of directions,
irritations, wrinkles,

a scatter of points
too rapid to see
straight-on.

Imagine
dipping your toes
into that tension

like poking your finger
into electricity,
pulled into something

so transparent you see
yourself beneath you
toe to toe and know

nothing holds you up
holds you down
but the dance

of atoms
that   at a distance,
lose even their name —

a glittering matrix
of lights
under leaf shadow.

Kelp after Storm

Look at these limbs
piled high against the sea wall.
On the smeared sand
a bone with roots exposed,
here a brain,
something cudgelled
to a knobbled cosh.
They flap wet leather straps
unbuckled.

I have never known
a beach of bones.
In the cave I wade
knee-deep, feel them
splitting beneath my feet,
hauled up as if the sea,
sickened of this spongy breakage,
shoved dark spaces
fist-full.

One arm pokes up
a mute entreat,
the hand of a child,
small stubborn flag.
I hold it.

Section Two: Learning to Swim

Learning to Swim

Every Sunday in the pool
on Water Street
my brother and me with you,
no others —

the cool of water
drying a chlorine film on skin,
and our voices
echoing.

I don't remember the moment
when you finally let go,
which is strange.
I remember you pushing away

my two-wheel bike,
my fiercely frightened joy.
I remember the last time
you said goodbye.

But in the pool on Water Street,
what I remember
is your index finger
supporting me on my stomach,

floating, a small, mesmerised island
above your finger,
told to trust the membrane
holding me up, and my focus —

total — on you, your finger
like a promise, the strong stem
roping the lily
into place in a pond.

The Shed

I'm about four,
suddenly aware —
stepping out of the back door
off the step where my grandmother
sits with a bucket
showing me green peas
nubs sweet against my teeth
how to open a pod
'whoo whoo'
in between our voices
the collared dove
sun warm on my cheeks
on the crazy paving
on the pattern of edges
I jump —

now I am running
down the path to the shed
at the bottom of the garden
where it's dark
opening the door
there on the wall above me
an angel —
her gold head, shoulders and wings
a glory of dust motes —
staring straight ahead
shining.
That's all there is —
it stops here
at the doorway.

The Light

A child is in the bed.
Light falls from the lamp in the yard
on the chair — the rounded back,
the sturdy legs
but the seat is in shadow.
The dressing-gown hangs
a body from the door.
In the washbasin
light skates a cold varnish,
fixes the bowl to its black hole.

There are places it cannot reach.

Over the linoleum
it pulls itself,
climbing each crease and curve,
probes fingers in the slivers
of shadow in between,
creeps over slippers by the bed
where there is someone else
in there with the child.

On the wall it flares, pressing the black back.

There is rain falling,
a soft plip-plipping
on the sill,
the flake of paint and plaster
giving way to the dark wet
that waits
around the lamp's heavy head.

Initiation

My mother gave me pads with pins.
I liked their wodged thickness
the drag-down drip of blood
blotted in something soft,
big like a body pressed warm
between my legs.

I liked my smell, sharp-edged,
iron filings licked but sweet
with the pooling damp of salty skin,
snail-traces of something dissolving —
the shock and shine
of what's inside.

But it's not allowed:
the tangy cloud
lingering around me by tea-time.

I remember the bathroom,
leg up, the cartoon girl
on the back of the box
pony-tailed, smiling, sliding a tube
so neatly between two pencil lines,
my dry heat, the soreness of my eyes
rain falling on the fells outside

voices behind the door chanting
have you done it yet?

Autumn Equinox on Mattiscombe Beach

We walk there in before-dark light,
black rock breaking the sea's drive,
not a soul on the gleaming wet
shift and slide of shingle.
Beyond the Horse's Head
sky blots gold.
We scoop out sand,
search for stones.

You light the fire, I watch you.
The sky deepens
rocks soften
I remember we slept here years ago.
I remember you making a line in the sand
that you stepped over.

There is no moon,
only the dark
snaring the earth's waters,
a gold orchestra heating our faces,
breaking a nail in a splutter of sparks.

When night and day
hang equal in our hands
I feel my way to the sea
cold around my feet,
look back at your face
rimmed on the fire's edge.

Wood turns molten,
fingers of flame retreat into red caves —
time to scatter the embers.
A billion pulsing points
spark and die beneath our feet:
we leave the universe
burning in the sand.

Survival

Since you left I talk to myself all the time.
It's not your voice: less calming, less critical,
but it is essential, the way you were.

It hasn't sprung up to disturb the silence
but rather, to quieten the pandemonium
that's broken out in your absence.

Winter Solstice at Easedale Tarn

On the grass, cold wind roughing me up,
I remembered what I'd forgotten —
we were here for your birthday
sitting on that hummock opposite.
We crossed the stream to reach it,
the wind rocked us then but the Spring sun,
brilliant, fitful, caught your face
half-turned towards me laughing,
oddly elfin, not quite human,
eyes crinkled and clever like your father's.

The water shone like corrugated metal
and one lone seagull surfed the ripples.
We ate a picnic, waded back
across the stream into the rest of your day.
I'd forgotten. But that hummock,
squatly folded over the water
suddenly releases us, vivid and solid
as the stones under my feet.
Wet wind, the shifting sheets of sky
flapping up the valley —
there we are on the opposite side.

And here I am, eight months on,
adrift as a ghost.
I must meet us on that hill
but can't cross the rain-freighted stream
tipping itself out of the tarn
like something unplugged.

I can only watch us leaving.
Already the stream was rising,
already the sky was turning to stone
and the way ahead — I think you knew it —
was blocked.

Homecoming

The house won't know you.
You think it will,
putting your key in the lock that sticks,
walking into the room you haven't seen for months
but there's a dark seep of wet on the ceiling
and what is that chair in the corner?
That was never there.

The hallway feels small — smaller than before
as if the house is pressing itself away from you
shrinking inwards, but you get through,
banging your bags against the walls
seeing out of the corner of your eye
the old photographs, those faces
blooming out of the ruins like pale flowers.

But it's through the next door that you feel it —
something askew,
as if the whole room has shifted slightly
out of its body, not solid,
not quite sitting in its outlines
but dislodged, as if every single thing
knows itself watched and watches you.

You look round
but there's a high whine in your ears
something off-balance that flickers
at the edge of your gaze
as if the sea is coming in
under the floorboards
like it did ninety years ago.

You will go up the stairs
not knowing when you open that door
who will be at the desk looking up,
startled. It will be dusk outside
again, the whole house lit up
your desk-lamp printing
another face on the dark window.

Father

I see him now
standing full-square in the kitchen
pressing the room back with his weight
his heavy-set exuberance.
Hit me here he'd say, feet planted apart,
pushing his stomach out. It wasn't his belly
but his diaphragm he thrust at me —
who only came up to his chest —
that convex round of muscle,
confident as a tight-stretched drum.
Hit me here he'd order, so I would,
tentatively, not wanting to hurt.
I remember my fist on shirt,
the laundered, warm Old Spice smell of him,
the gin-and-tonic sweetness of his breath.
No! Harder! he'd laugh, and so it was
I pushed through my reluctance
like puncturing a skin
and punched with all my strength
again and again, feeling my knuckles land
on something smooth, hard as a shield,
hearing his laugh — my impermeable father,
his voice inside a fortress
and, watchful sentinel on the counter,
the never-empty glass of gin and tonic
keeping time.

The Room

I didn't know that time was the last time
the last chance dissolving downwards.
Every month the tacit choice made
and blood, clotty, metallic
the consequence.

Now, I miss my ripeness —
heavy and fragile, easily bruised,
the deep urge of the room
its doors wide open,
the ache of the room still empty.

This room was created for someone
who never came —
whose curtailment again and again
bled like a wound
quiet, uncomplaining.

It's contracting now,
darkness resigned to itself.
Had I known it was the last time
I'd have made the same choice
but entered, paused,

looked around, and knelt —
honoured this room for its patience,
exquisite preparation, attention to detail,
generosity — so open,
ready, beautiful.

I would have spoken aloud
what I was growing in a different soil.
I would have left flowers and incense,
blessings sweet as blood
behind the closed door.

Visiting my Father

At first, all I see is the box.

There is a man in the box.
He fills it. No room to spare.
He could wiggle his toes but
no room to fling out his arms
roll on to his side or kick his legs.
I don't recognise him.

That's not true.
I know who I've come to see
but his face is not there.
Who is this with his mask
set dead-still,
prominent nose slightly hooked

it seems, nothing really out of place
yet all features alien —
like a photograph of the cat
caught in a snarl, or the child
mid-scream; this is *it*,
the final still-frame.

Then I see
he's wearing a pink dress
satin, a sort of shift:
necked, sleeved,
straight to his feet.

Imagine, our final meeting
before you are lidded up
and consigned to the flames
being this:

you are boxed
and wearing a pink dress,
presented to me
like a sepulchral rose.

All Hallows Eve / Samhain

Last night I lit candles for the dead,
in the fire's light ignited small fires.
Each one brought close to my mouth
heard what was never said
what has been said many times.

I did not begin with an order
but they came in formation of a sort,
the ones who left the biggest gaps
then the ones missed at the edge,
such a press of them suddenly

waiting for a flame,
each carrying a story —
seeing for the first time
how many have left,
a constellation of absence —

how full the room felt
behind me.

Section Three: My Mother's Language

My Mother's Language

In the early morning, as the tide pulls back,
her first sounds wheel and fidget on the foreshore

getting their bearings: *where-why-what*
pick-pick of scavengers tearing at weed,

turning over pebbles, throwing up a crab-claw,
hunting for the left-behind

titbits in the dislocated kelp
flung on the tideline.

By lunchtime she knows, like the gulls,
there is something there under the flotsam

of discarded cups, a tangle of ropes,
a bloated shoe, each half-known thing

unearthed carefully, held up for an instant
to the light — and dropped.

What is that unrecognisable thing
out on the water? Under a million stones

small words scuttle out of sight,
and out of the frightening sky

a cloud-shift quenches the afternoon light,
makes even the shallowest pool

impenetrable. In the puddled sand
a mystified calligraphy of webbed feet

circles the same phrases over again
and she reaches the sea

more by chance — sinks down
under the waves' heave.

In the Sadness of Spring

my mother chews the gravelly bread
of memory, hunting meaning's nub,
retreats to the comfort-cud of repetition.

In the sadness of Spring
in the luminous dusk
she grasps for thought-holds

that crumble — flails in the terrored space —
catches a child's words,
pulls on the lifeline of my still-remembered love.

As she folds the clipped wings
of her cardigan round her,
sits, shifts, recoils

from the bright insistent grab of questions
without answers,
I see her face change —

pulling the hood over her eyes,
her features sharpen.
Something older peers out

from the bony-shouldered dark —
beaked, benignly empty,
appraising the land that's gone to waste.

Skylark

Let's stop, you say.
We get out of the car into Summer.
The lane dreams bees
in a blue ache of sky,
a humming filigree of flowers.

Listen, a skylark! I say.
Excitement brightens your face
like a child swinging open
the door to an empty room,
singing.

We look up —
see the blurry-feathered dot
swallowed in light,
a down-shimmer
of disembodied song.

You stand, holding the car-door,
smiling.
The moment has come
(I never know when it's coming)
side-stepping you

out of illness,
washing you in its urgent beauty,
                    now, now —
I see you
brought back by a skylark.

Ropes

Summer — sun pressing against the window
like a child denied attention.
The fire is on, 'The King and I'
choruses its story.

Do you remember?
lobbing memories like ropes
begging a catch.
Yes I do!

Your smile returns you
so that even now
six years disappear —
singing *Getting to Know You*

as I knead the bumps
and cracks in your feet,
resting in my hands
like broken birds.

And I wonder who's clinging to whom —
you, grasping at the parts
of yourself I throw towards you,
or me, watching

your frantic eyes go under,
scrabbling in the wreckage
for something, anything
to keep you afloat.

By every bedside
in every airless room
so many, half-in, half-out,
flail beseeching hands

and those of us on the edge
hear our voices pleading
let go! let go!
all the time throwing ropes.

The Night Call

Your mother's upset
the carer said on the phone.
I can't get her to bed.
So I went. It was about nine at night,
the cul de sac was quiet,
lamp-lit, all the windows closed.

When I walk in, my mother
is circling the hall, shaking off
the carer's hands. *They're out there*
she says, *my children,*
all alone and it's night.
They're only young. Let me go,
let me find them.

She pushes away my soothing arms
and my words fall off her.
Around and around she circles,
struggling for the door,
brute strength
in her desperation.

Back in the car, I dial her landline
from my mobile
and there, in the waiting dark,
a tiny-child voice grows out of my throat.
Mummy? I say.

I tell her we are all right —
staying with our Daddy —
we will see her tomorrow.

Her voice quietens.
Are you sure you're safe? she asks.
Yes, I reply
and sit there in the silent street
where, at the edge of the street lamp's glow
our three small shapes —

brother, sister, me —
stand just out of sight.

The Lift Opens

into the corridor and sometimes
you're right there, rapping an urgent question
on the nurses' window

or turning back down the corridor
unanswered, hauling the rail
like someone blind in a cave.

Often I find you in someone else's room,
the nurse, clipped, kind,
directing you out

but there's no *out*, *in*
mine or *not mine*,
no signs to map you to ground.

Now, I stand at the lounge door
you in an armchair
a collapse of cardigan and cushions

and comprehension pauses
at the tableau: nursing home,
the warm, sweet, rancid seep

of cooked food, trapped air,
tang of urine, the stain
something cellular.

It's always the same: coming up
to the edge of your world,
gentlest touch of finger

to paper-vellum cheek
and waiting — everything suspended —
for that light to fly up

from deepest space in your eyes
breaking the atmosphere
in a flood of recognition

when you say my name.

The Waves

It won't be long now
before the waves come
my mother says, staring

through my shoulder.
The what? I ask.
She repeats it,

a touch impatient
and I see them
in her room at night

a bright oscillation
across the walls
towards her bed

pulsing over the carpet,
crests alight. Will she turn
towards them

will her eyes be open?
I follow her gaze
to the living room door.

Beyond the dark glass
they heave
waiting to break.

When will they come?
I ask.
I don't know.

She is beached somewhere
doesn't need questions
but I need to know.

What are they like?
She smiles
rare light

Oh they're sweet
she says.

Another Place

In this room time slows
to the drip drip
of tea, biscuits, pills

advancing trolley wheels
the discreet knock,
an endless bleep.

A torpor, thick and heavy,
anaesthetic, seeps through me
but not you.

You drag your distress
to the edge of the chasm
at your feet

over and over again,
waking me up to see you,
dark silhouette

framed in panic's bright filaments.
My reassurances fall around you
useless as dead birds.

But there is one way
to bring you and me
to another place.

I take you to bed,
watch your slow collapsing
bone by bone,

a litany of whimpers
bringing you close to my side.
Now, sometimes,

we can sleep at last,
the wisp of your hair's drift
on my cheek, your sour breath

suspended in the air
like a blessing.
I hold your hands. Wait.

Aren Zoeken

Dutch expression pertaining to the dying, meaning
'looking for the seed-heads of grains'

My mother is gleaning.
One hand moves slowly,

carefully, over the duvet
forefinger and thumb

feeling their way — pausing —
now picking something up

and holding it — suspended —
in the air

before forefinger and thumb
separate, release their unseen seed

and recommence
their search across the bed

or sometimes across her own arm
in its nightdress sleeve.

I watch her, watching this
last harvesting. She observes

her hand as if it is something
apart from her.

Her cataract-dulled eyes
are intent.

The room is still
save for this ritual act

following its own logic
inexorably as the seasons

for this is the time of last pickings —
retrieving the tiny seed-heads

left behind after life,
hidden beneath broken stalks

in the exhausted soil
that is ready to sleep.

Dementia

It's called a drift down
or a sinking into

but it's a journey out —
of the self, of your world

constructed meticulously
over thousands of days,

your memory-web festooned
with countless keepsakes

where the 'I' hangs,
held in place by innumerable threads

where *me* and *our* and *us*
span outwards from the centre,

all of them connected, and at dawn
when *I* wakes to the world,

whatever the season,
the web shimmers in light

in that precise blessing
of life embodied.

Not now.

Around the space
where you once were

we gather your relics
in mourning

while you look on
knowing that what you witness

is charged with terrible meaning,
having no idea why.

Section Four: To Make a Path

To Make a Path

you have to stroke your face
from scalp to chin
over and over again
and as you do, you know
you are pulling the path down
from the top of your head.
It will feel like ruffled silk,
a little resistant to your pull
which is not really a pull
more of a stroking
into being but insistent,
spooling out of your head.
You have to trust it is coming,
flowing downwards over your face.
I do not know what colour it is,
only you know that
and I do not know where it will go
or how you will use it. Perhaps
it will float outwards, attaching
itself to branches, so that
you can find your way home
in the dark, or it may settle
on the ground
so that when you walk out
in your bare feet you will hear
the quiet hum of your soul,
the air pockets of your thoughts
between your toes.

Making a Drum

Start with the birchwood ring,
a hole full of something not yet manifest.
Scroll your paintbrush round its inner rim
where your name will vibrate a secret frequency.

Smooth the ring with sandpaper.
Now for the skin, hallowed and pale as a moon,
damp as dough,
full moon and full eclipse together —
perfectly round but hidden until it is dry.
Punch holes in it.

Lay it flat on top of your ring
slippery between your fingers,
      and suddenly you see her
      against the sky to your side,
for you cannot touch a skin
and not call the spirit.
She moves closer —
visceral, musky,
as you stretch the skin across the frame
stretching and turning, pulling her over the ring.

Be patient. Already the skin is drying.
Run your hands across its lunar surface,
its left-behind hairs brush against your fingers, silver or dark
      there she is again on your eye-edge, sunlit flanks.
When the skin is tight and smooth
turn it face down.
Take the thin wet rope of sinewy thread,
lace it through the holes.

Pull and turn, coaxing the tissues just enough apart
to let in the wind of the moor, dark cloud,
a den of bracken —
then wait three days

as your drum unveils its face
of browns, golds and creams,
bars and splashes, scars.

Pick up your beater
            — bring it down
and something will break
inside you, the last-instant echo
of panicked hooves,
a momentary shudder —
red deer is home.

Aisha

In memory of Aisha Ibrahim Duhulow, who was stoned to death in October 2008 by a group of 50 men in a stadium in Kismayo, Somalia, in front of around 1000 spectators. She was accused of adultery but had in fact been raped by 3 men. She was 13 years old.

The small bulb of your head
pokes above ground —
not to grow but to crack
like an egg broken open.

You see them coming from all sides —
perhaps close your eyes,
your eyes slam shut.
Your face turns on its stem
towards the red flood —
each fold and curve smooth-warm.

Thirteen long circles of the patient sun
cup the sum of your mystery, perfect.
In that moment, earth holds you
before the first stone,

the intaken breath of a thousand stares
that takes them over the humming edge
of frenzy, the shuddering space
where they will not see your face.

Later — lifted out of the earth and checked —
your young pulse thuds
its stubborn refusal.
Returned to the ground,
what's begun has to end
in the dark wet wreckage of red dust.

What's left —
the stillness of stones still sticky,
the scrambling tumult of your blood,
each cell spinning you onto rock,

the stillness of stones
across which your dark hairs' signature
thick as spider's silk
fixes the gleam of your name
to the earth's face.

Night in the Arctic Circle

Beyond the dipped head
of the last streetlamp
spilling recognition
there is something else
we do not know is there
until we reach it —

a silence recognised
after death when
what is ahead
cannot be known
only stepped into —

vast, cognisant
a face I am a breath away from.

On either side white trees
in deep freeze
hold the stillness
of their massed dream,
white snow creaks
beneath my feet
shadow-tracked in animals.

There is nothing dead here
only suspension —
the dark road ahead
starred black
and cold —

and I imagine the men
leaving the lit tent
when it was not howling
but still, dark,
white snow lighting the dark,
stars and this vast face
waiting —

a surrendering
not failure or fear
but trust infinitely young
shrugging off all edges
all separation
walking towards it.

St Raphael's Chapel, Huccaby

For Chris

So many times we would talk prayer: how we did it, who to.
Now, in this chapel on the moor, old stones dissolving
to daffodils, droplets of blackbird-song,
I sit in the first pew and talk to you.

How come you're suddenly the addressee?
How come the silent listener now
and not sitting beside me, emphatic finger
jabbing at my uncertainty?

It's not hard to hear you listening, acerbic at times,
not hard to know you're all right.
But I don't know how you stepped over —
became in the space of a stopped breath

one of that circle of observers I call out to.
In one moment, when all moments ceased,
your senses extended, curling and sparking,
beyond decayed flesh into this,

that I believe watches, cares —
that I have to believe cares.

The wood is hard against my legs,
the air thick with polleny breath,
the last exhalations of Easter flowers
dropping themselves into silence.

Gull Dawn

Long after I have left
I will remember the gulls
carrying dawn to me,

the ragged wires of their voices
slowly skewering my dreams open.
I am tuned to that sound

of something calling its name over and over
bringing themselves back
into bone, beak, wings, claws

as they fly out of their dark roost
                here they come across
the dragon-tail of rock

as the sky flushes open,
calling the sun up over the horizon.

Oversteps Books Ltd

The Oversteps list includes books by the following poets:

David Grubb, Giles Goodland, Alex Smith, Will Daunt, Patricia Bishop, Christopher Cook, Jan Farquarson, Charles Hadfield, Mandy Pannett, Doris Hulme, James Cole, Helen Kitson, Bill Headdon, Avril Bruton, Marianne Larsen, Anne Lewis-Smith, Mary Maher, Genista Lewes, Miriam Darlington, Anne Born, Glen Phillips, Rebecca Gethin, W H Petty, Melanie Penycate, Andrew Nightingale, Caroline Carver, John Stuart, Rose Cook, Jenny Hope, Hilary Elfick, Anne Stewart, Oz Hardwick, Terry Gifford, Michael Swan, Maggie Butt, Anthony Watts, Robert Stein, Graham High, Ross Cogan, Ann Kelley, A C Clarke, Diane Tang, R V Bailey, John Daniel, Alwyn Marriage, Kathleen Kummer, Jean Atkin, Charles Bennett, Elisabeth Rowe, Marie Marshall, Ken Head, Robert Cole, Cora Greenhill, John Torrance, Michael Bayley, Christopher North, Simon Richey, Lynn Roberts, Sue Davies, Mark Totterdell, Michael Thomas, Ann Segrave, Helen Overell, Rose Flint, Denise Bennett, James Turner, Sue Boyle, Jane Spiro, Jennie Osborne, John Daniel, Janet Loverseed, Wendy Klein, Sally Festing, Angela Stoner, Simon Williams, Susan Taylor, Richard Skinner, Fokkina McDonnell, Joan McGavin and David Broadbridge.

For details of all these books, information about Oversteps and up-to-date news, please look at our website and blog:

www.overstepsbooks.com
http://overstepsbooks.wordpress.com